CW00850840

Threads books in hardback

Beans	Plastics
Bread	Rice
Bricks	Rocks
Clay	Salt
Cotton	Silk
Eggs	Spices
Fruit	Tea
Glass	Water
Milk	Wood
Paper	Wool

First paperback edition 1991

First published 1987 in hardback by
A & C Black (Publishers) Limited
35 Bedford Row, London WC1R 4JH

ISBN 0–7136–3501–0

Copyright © 1991, 1987 A & C Black (Publishers) Ltd

A CIP catalogue record for this book
is available from the British Library.

Acknowledgements
Illustrations by Caroline Ewen
Photographs by Chris Fairclough, except for p 9 Milk Marketing Board;
p 14 R. T. Phillips.

The author and the publisher would like to thank the staff at Marchant's Hill
Rural Studies Centre and the pupils of Langbourne School for their help and
cooperation.

Typeset by August Filmsetting, Haydock, St Helens
Printed in Belgium by Proost International Book Production

Milk

Annabelle Dixon

Photographs by Chris Fairclough

Contents

A&C Black · London

Is this why you drink milk?

There's always some about.

It tastes nice.

You might drink milk for any of these reasons, but the last one is the most important. When you are growing, milk helps to make your bones strong and gives you energy.

Milk may just look like white runny stuff, but it's much more interesting than that.

It's cold.

It's good for me.

I like it.

Rice pudding

Fruit yoghurt

Pancakes

Milk in our food

We don't only drink milk, we eat it in our food, too.

We can use it to make sweet foods, like rice pudding, kulfi, fruit yoghurt, burfi, cakes or biscuits . . .

. . . or savoury foods, like Yorkshire pudding, cheese, dumplings or pancakes.

These are just a few. Can you think of any other kinds of food which are made with milk?

Burfi

Yorkshire pudding

Kulfi

Dumplings

Macaroni chee

Biscuits

Where does milk come from?

The milk we buy in bottles or cartons usually comes from cows. When a cow has a baby, she makes milk in her body for the baby to drink. This calf is sucking milk from its mother.

Lots of other animal mothers, like goats, mice and cats, make milk for their babies to drink. Animals which do this are called mammals and each kind of mammal makes a slightly different type of milk which is best for her own young.

We are mammals, and the very best food for human babies is their own mother's milk.

Cows, goats, sheep and buffaloes are all kept by farmers for their milk. Look in a shop that sells milk and cheese and see if you can find some which come from different animals.
Try tasting them with your eyes shut.
Can you guess which ones you are tasting?

Not so long ago, many people used to keep their own animals to give them milk. Some people still do.

This cow is being milked by hand. The woman curls her fingers around one of the cow's teats, and pulls and squeezes until a jet of milk comes out. Nowadays, most cows are milked by machines which do the job of pulling and squeezing the cow's teats.

Do you want to try what it feels like to milk an animal? Find an old pair of rubber gloves. Fill one with water and tie it very tightly around the wrist.

With a darning needle, prick a hole in the end of each finger. These will be the 'teats'. Ask a friend to hold the glove over a bucket or sink.

Now curl your fingers round a 'teat' and pull and squeeze until a jet of water comes out. You may need to practise.

7

How does milk get to us?

We usually buy our milk from the shops, or the milkman delivers it to us.

Have you ever noticed the milkman writing things down in a book? This is his order book and he has to fill it in correctly so that he gives everyone the right amount of milk and the right bill at the end of the week.

Could you design your own order book? How would you plan it?

The milkmen get their milk from depots. Early in the mornings, they collect crates of milk bottles from the depots and load them on to their vans or milk floats.

The milk is delivered to the depot from a dairy. At the dairy, the milk has been tested to make sure that it is clean and fresh, and then put into bottles or cartons by machine.

Each dairy puts its own design on the milk bottles and cartons. On some cartons, there are facts about the kind of milk inside. Have a look at some cartons and bottles and see what's written on them. Imagine you own a dairy. Can you design your own milk cartons and bottles?

9

How does the milk get to the dairies? It is usually delivered to them by milk tankers that go round collecting the milk from dairy farms each day.

Not so long ago, milk was collected from farms in metal containers, called churns. Now, it is easier for farmers to keep the milk in large storage tanks and then pump it into the milk tankers.

Keeping milk clean

The tanker driver and the farmer both have to be very careful to keep the milk clean and fresh.

Very small living things, called bacteria, use milk as their food if they can get into it. Some bacteria are harmless, some are even useful, but if we drink milk that the wrong kind of bacteria have got into, it can make us ill.

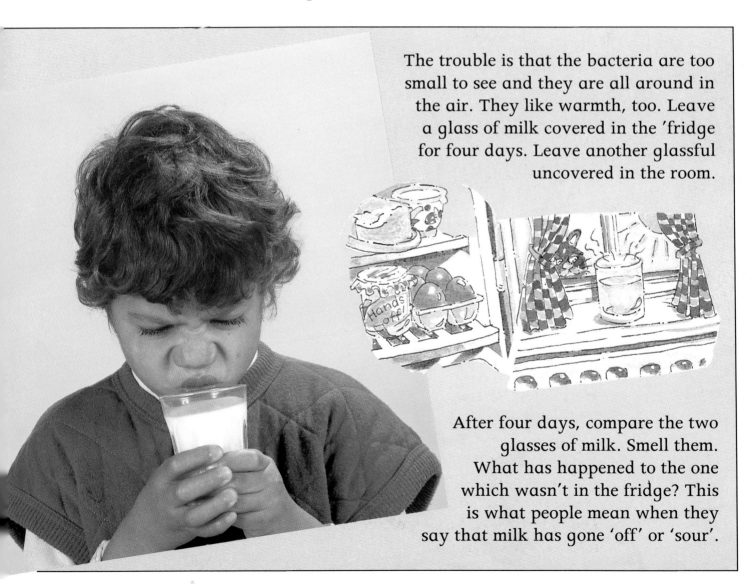

The trouble is that the bacteria are too small to see and they are all around in the air. They like warmth, too. Leave a glass of milk covered in the 'fridge for four days. Leave another glassful uncovered in the room.

After four days, compare the two glasses of milk. Smell them. What has happened to the one which wasn't in the fridge? This is what people mean when they say that milk has gone 'off' or 'sour'.

The farmer has to make sure that the milk is kept clean from the time the cows are milked to the time when the milk goes into the tanker.

Farmworkers have to wash their hands.

They have to wash the cows down each time they are milked.

The milk goes from the milking machines through pipes to the storage tank next door. The farmworkers have to wash all the machines every milking time so that no stale milk is left in them.

The milking parlour, the shed where the cows are milked, also has to be washed down.

Can you find the things which need washing in this picture?

Although the farmers are very careful, there is still a chance that some tiny bacteria may get into the milk. A famous Frenchman, called Louis Pasteur, was the first person to realise that the harmful bacteria would have to be killed to stop people from becoming ill. He found out that if milk was heated quickly to a very high temperature, the bacteria could be killed. Now, all milk has to be treated at the farm, or at the dairy before it is sold for drinking.

13

Milk and cream

Just as there are lots of different kinds of dogs or horses, there are also many different types of cows. These are two kinds you often see.

▲ **Jersey cows** (or Channel Island cows) give very creamy milk.

◄ **Fresian cows** give more milk than Jersey cows, but their milk has less cream in it.

You can find these different sorts of milk in the shops, but if you look at the labels, you'll see that the cream is called butterfat. Milk with high butterfat is very creamy. Milk with hardly any cream, or with the cream taken off is called skimmed milk. What do you think semi-skimmed means?

If the label says that the milk is 5% butterfat, it means that in every 100 spoonfuls of milk, there are 5 spoonfuls of cream. If the label says 11% butterfat, there are 11 spoonfuls of cream in every 100 spoons of milk.

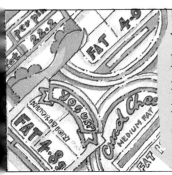

With your friends, make a collection of different kinds of milk. You can take a notebook to copy the names down when you go shopping. Which kind of milk has the highest amount of butterfat? Does it say anything about fat on yoghurt or cheese labels?

What can you make from milk?

Lots of different kinds of food, like cheese, butter, ghee, yoghurt and junket, are made from milk. Most of these foods are now made in factories, but you can still try to do it the home-made way.

Try making a simple cheese

You will need

A refrigerator

A large tub
of full-fat plain yoghurt

A clean cloth

A rubber band, or string

A large basin

How to do it

1. Very carefully pour out the yoghurt into a large, clean cloth. Pull the ends of the cloth together to make a bag, and put some string or a rubber band round the neck of the bag. Hang it over a basin for 3 or 4 days, until it has stopped dripping. You can give it a *gentle* squeeze to help it along.

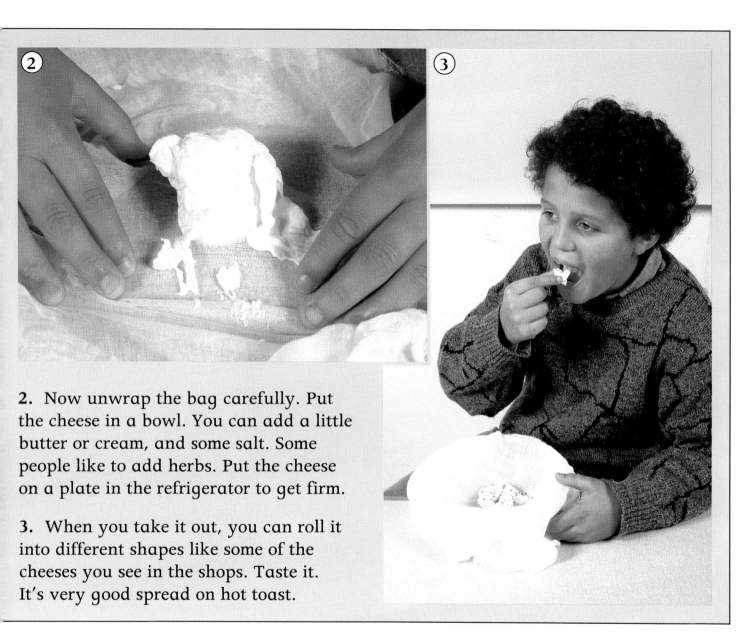

2. Now unwrap the bag carefully. Put the cheese in a bowl. You can add a little butter or cream, and some salt. Some people like to add herbs. Put the cheese on a plate in the refrigerator to get firm.

3. When you take it out, you can roll it into different shapes like some of the cheeses you see in the shops. Taste it. It's very good spread on hot toast.

You have made a soft cheese. Hard cheeses, like Cheddar, take much longer to make. On the last page of this book, you can find out how to make a hard cheese.

Cheese has been made for hundreds of years. Before refrigerators were invented, it was hard to stop milk from going 'off' too quickly. Cheese was a very useful way of storing the goodness of milk.

Try making butter

You will need

A refrigerator

568 ml of fresh full-fat milk

Channel Island milk is good for this recipe. Can you guess why?

A clean container with a screw-top lid

A sieve

A bowl

Some paper towel

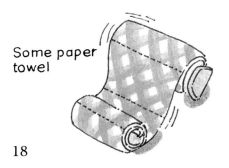

① EST TIMES

How to do it

1. Pour the milk into the container. Screw on the lid tightly and shake for at least 20 minutes. After a while, you will see yellow blobs of butter starting to appear in the milk.

18

2. Keep shaking until you get bigger lumps of butter. Lay your paper towel over a sieve. Open the container and pour the milk carefully through the sieve into a bowl. You can drink the milk afterwards. It is called buttermilk.

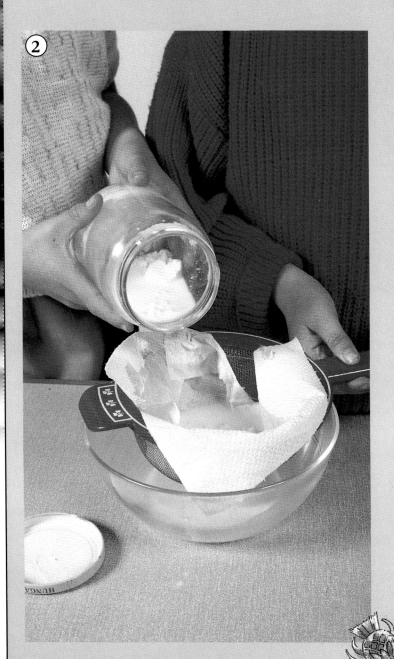

3. Pick up the paper towel with the butter on and put it on a plate in the refrigerator. When the butter is cold, you can press the bits together to make one big piece. People who still make their own butter use wooden pats to do this. Sometimes they cut their own design on to a pat.
Try designing a butter mark or pat of your own.

You can make ghee from butter

You will need

115 grammes of butter

A small saucepan

A sieve

A jar

Some paper towel

A hot-plate or cooker

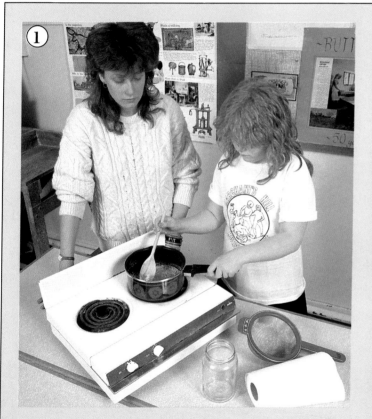

How to do it

1. Warm the butter very gently in a pan until it has melted.

2. Line the sieve with paper towel or a paper coffee filter. Pour the melted butter through it, into the jar. The white bits in the butter should stay on the paper, they are called milk solids. The liquid in the jar is ghee, it is used for deep-frying vegetables or meat. Out of the refrigerator, ghee keeps much longer than butter.

Make your own yoghurt

You will need

A tablespoon
of plain *live* yoghurt

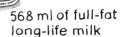

568 ml of full-fat
long-life milk

A saucepan

A hot-plate
or cooker

A thermos (or a large jar with a screw top
and a warm place like an airing cupboard)

How to do it

1. Heat the milk very slowly in a saucepan, don't let it boil.

2. Pour it carefully into the thermos or jar, nearly up to the top.

3. Add the tablespoon of yoghurt and stir gently. Yoghurt has some 'friendly' bacteria in it and they do the work of turning milk into yoghurt.

4. Screw on the top of your container and leave it for one or two days (in a warm place if you are using a jar). When you open it up, you should have nice creamy yoghurt. Try it with some of your favourite jam.

21

Storing milk

Yoghurt and cheese are two different ways of storing the goodness of milk. Do you know any other ways?

Condensed milk has sugar added to it. Bacteria don't like sugar, so they will only grow very slowly. Bacteria need air, too. If the condensed milk is sealed in a tin, the bacteria won't grow at all.

You can make your own condensed milk, but it takes practice.

You will need

A hot-plate

284 ml of full cream milk

or cooker

A saucepan

4 tablespoons of sugar

How to do it

1. Put the milk and sugar in a saucepan and, very slowly, bring them to the boil. Now turn down the heat as low as it will go. Keep cooking the milk until it looks thick and creamy.

2. Pour it into a bowl. Cover the bowl and leave it for four days. Has it gone sour?

Here are some other ways of storing milk.

Ultra high temperature (or UHT milk). Milk is heated quickly to very high temperatures, which kills all the bacteria. When you open a box of UHT milk, you let in air and new bacteria, and the milk will then go off.

Dried milk. There are many ways of drying milk into a powder. Nowadays, factories freeze-dry milk, using special machines. The water in the milk is driven off by being frozen quickly at very low temperatures.

Evaporated milk. Milk is cooked slowly without any sugar until it becomes very creamy. It is then sealed into tins so that no air can get in.

With your friends, make a collection of these kinds of milk. Blindfold each other in turn, and see if you can tell which kind of stored milk you are tasting.

Look at some dried milk powder. Feel it in your fingers. This is what is left when all the water has been taken out of milk. The milk powder is made of what are called milk solids.

Milk solids are often used in foods made in factories. Look at the labels on packets of biscuits, or soup tins, chocolates and cake mixes. You may be surprised by some of the different foods which have milk solids in them.

Milk solids are often used in animal foodstuffs, and they are also used to make paints and glues.

Look again at your glass of milk. There has been a lot to find out about something that looks so simple.

More things to do

1. What else can you make with milk? Try to find recipes for rice pudding or sevian, lassi, ice cream, tzatziki or custard.

2. Try making a hard cheese. Do you remember the rhyme about Miss Muffet who was eating 'curds' and 'whey'? You get curds and whey when you make this cheese.

You will need: 4 pints of full cream milk; clean muslin or kitchen 'J' cloth; a large yoghurt pot with a hole in the bottom; a plate which fits inside the yoghurt pot; one dessertspoon of salt; a small bottle of rennet (from the chemist); a heavy weight; a table knife; a large saucepan; a sieve or ladle with holes in.

How to do it: Clean your pot and line it with a 'J' cloth or muslin. Put about $\frac{1}{2}$ teaspoon of rennet (no more) into an eggcup full of water. Heat the milk in a saucepan until it feels very warm (about 90°F). Stir in the rennet very slowly, *don't* let the milk boil. Let the milk cool for one hour; it will turn into a soft jelly, called junket. Cut this carefully into small pieces.

Heat the milk very slowly again. Drain off the watery part (this is the whey). Put the rest (the curds) into the yoghurt pot, add the salt, and fold the cloth over the top. Put a small plate on top of the cheese and weigh it down with the heavy weight. Leave for two days, then turn the cheese out of the pot on to a new cloth. Keep the cheese in a dry place and turn it over every day for two weeks. Then it will be ready to eat.

3. If you live in a town, try to find out if there is a city farm nearby where you can see a cow or a goat being milked.

4. Watch out for your local milkman. What does it say on his milk float? Try making a map for a milk round in your area.

Index